T0130060

SUSAN'S BEDTIME STORIES

Susan Picosa

iUniverse, Inc.
Bloomington

Susan's Bedtime Stories

iUniverse books may be ordered through booksellers or by contacting:

iUniverse
1663 Liberty Drive
Bloomington, IN 47403
www.iuniverse.com
1-800-Authors (1-800-288-4677)

ISBN: 978-1-4759-3718-3 (sc)

Printed in the United States of America

iUniverse rev. date: 07/06/2012

About the Author

Susan Picosa is a successful artist/designer living in Washington D.C. Her aesthetic excellence has continually put her in contact with many famous and talented men over the years, leading to her being *in touch* with them on an ongoing basis . . . who could ask for anything more if you know what that means.

Introduction

I wrote this book for all of those who have not yet realized what they might have been missing. Try these stories on for size. My life is an open book. All you have to do is turn to page one, and I guarantee you will be delivered a steamy eye-opener of a read. Of course the names have been changed to protect the guilty. (You know who you are.)

My success with men comes partially because I've always given thought to the way I welcome someone into my home. For my lovers, I step it up a romantic notch by taking into consideration the individual essence of each new lover.

I also know how important it is to create a mood that is not just for the moment, but that lingers in a man's thoughts long after our lovemaking has ended for that day. This works for me, too. Whenever I reflect on those moments and recreate the scenario of our coming together, a warm smile comes across my lips and my breathing becomes a little faster-paced, almost as if I was right there again and loving it all once more.

As I recall the care that I have devoted to creating a warm and welcoming ambience for evening moments of sweet loving, flickering candlelight throughout the rooms always comes to mind. I can smell again the delicate fragrance of perfume wafting through the air, just enough to entice the senses of a loving fragrance.

I remember how my lover looked when he saw me appear in a beautiful white lace teddy, with a silk charmeuse evening coat casually draped over my body. I smile when I think of how each of my lovers knew what awaited him as I ushered him into my boudoir.

We both knew that things would progress from soft and sensual to hot and sizzling in the moments to follow. On sweet summer nights, my inviting wardrobe would be a gauze, sheer, floor-length spaghetti-strap dress, accompanied by a flowing open caftan in the same fabric. The breeze would blow through the fabric when I opened the front door, creating a gossamer effect like the fluttering of butterfly wings.

In these fondly-remembered scenarios, I've always been greeted with, "Oh, wow!"

With that I know that I am beauty in the eyes of the beholder. The confidence that my presentation instills in my lovers encourages the absolute care and wonderful energy that I know will generate an amazing time in our lovemaking with each other.

I hope my stories inspire the same for you. After reading my book, you might want to do a little shopping for yourself, once you've tried these stories on for size. I didn't have to return any of my merchandise, because it fit me really well, if you catch my drift. And if you don't catch it, read a few pages, and you will know exactly what I'm talking about!

Good feelings and feeling good becomes addictive. You want to experience them again and again.

~ Susan Picosa, April 2012

A Rhythm Deep Inside Me

I'd like to give you some understanding of where I've come from in my life. I was not always a free spirit as I am today. By allowing me to peel back the book's curtain just enough to give you a peek, you'll be able to take a look for yourself and go on this amazing journey with me.

Once upon a time, as I made a magical transformation from a Miss wide eyed doe to a soon to be Mrs. Life, everything seemed wonderful. I was told—by everyone who knew me well—that I had a smile that lit up the room. My days were filled with joyful thoughts and life's wonderful experiences. I felt as though I was dancing among the butterflies in fields of beautiful wildflowers. I had always been playful, sensitive, thoughtful, sensual, and saw life through the eyes of the true artist that I am in my heart and soul. My warmth and love of life touched all that I loved and those who loved me.

The first years of my marriage were full of joy and passion, but then things started to change. As time went on, I began to feel a deep sense of emotional neglect and romantic emptiness. It began to slowly permeate my spirit and negatively touched the very essence of my being.

I found myself longing to be kissed, and to share wonderful conversation. I was still a romantic young woman at the young age of 40. I had sexual desires from the top of my head down to the very tips of my toes, but they went unfulfilled.

When you are longing to be hugged, you develop a deep hunger to be nurtured and fed these loving emotions. In their absence, I felt as though there was a severe drought in my life. I was ready to put up a "Wanted" poster like in the old days of the Wild West. The heading would read "Wanted"—delicious hugs, drenching kisses, hot sex, sweet loving, more hot sex, and someone to make me feel like the woman that I really am!"

Simple words that would have meant everything— "You're really my best friend"—"You mean everything to me"—"I love you"—I never heard from my husband.

I felt increasingly that I was losing my identity and enduring the "I'm just fine" social posture, just to keep my marriage intact. My essence was slowly ebbing away. It's especially relevant for me today to paraphrase words from a song that holds special meaning for me: "There's a rhythm deep inside of you and you must get reacquainted." Speaking for myself I would add to that: "And I've been silent for too long."

What looked on the outside to my friends and family as me being perfectly fine, began to feel to me like I was living a lie of a life, and not being true to the true person that I am inside.

That "true to myself" personality started to peek through when I began my life anew as a single woman.

I began to realize that I was now ready to be deeply talked to, warmly hugged, drenchingly kissed, and very passionately loved up.

My name is Susan. Here is my story, and I'm ready to share it with all of you.

Jonathan Taylor

Let's begin with Mr. Jonathan Taylor. I met Jonathan at a nightclub in New York City. He was a tall, dark, elegant black man with a voice like creamy chocolate pudding. He swooned and crooned his way into success as a vocalist with one of the major orchestras. He was known as the bad boy of blues because he sang them like no one else has ever been able to replicate.

Jonathan Taylor sang from his soul, and from his life's experiences. He came up from difficult times, and evolved to becoming one of the world's greatest vocalists. When he opened his mouth to sing, people stopped everything and listened. When he spoke, people listened. He had a presence on stage and off that was undeniably profound.

He and I had something else going on. He called me his little shirt maker. I designed for him with delight, and I loved doing it. I was also his personal photographer for public appearances, and was able to capture his essence, like no other. These photographs touched him deeply, and he always cherished my creative abilities.

He also said to me, "Susan, never let anything out of your hot little hands without your signature." I've followed his instructions to the letter, and learned a lot from him. I must add that he always wore wonderful cologne by the name of "Grey Flannel" by Geoffrey Beene. I just loved being in his arms and inhaling the intoxicating scent of it and similarly, I always wear a perfume by the name of "Fracas" by Robert Piguet, that I call my signature fragrance. Jonathan and I always said that we could find each other in the dark without saying a word, just because we were so in tune with each other's fragrance.

Jonathan was an amazing person in my life, embracing me, introducing me to many other great jazz legends. At the time I was introduced by him, to a very important orchestra leader with whom he often worked, I began creating clothes for him and his wife as well He always especially appreciated me because travel time between shows could be very tight, and my clothing designs were of a fabric combination that could be hand-washed and ready to go the next morning. No more valet service, with a two-day turnaround for dry cleaning. I was heaven-sent to them, and paid very handsomely.

One day that I remember fondly, Jonathan had me stay over with him at the Waldorf-Astoria. He prepared a Jewish chicken soup that had so much pepper in it I could hardly breathe, but he tried, on how he tried. If he fell short on a culinary level, however, he made up for it in the romance department.

Jonathan and I had wonderful loving. He was very amply endowed and was very gentle and sweet in his loving of me, as was I with him. In the morning, the cool breeze blew through the beautiful hotel room curtains, and awakened us with delight. We would wrap ourselves in each other's arms and snuggle once again with a good morning kiss. I loved every beautiful moment.

Every time he came to town, it was a given that we would get together. I was always available when he called, as he was when I called him. It was an amazing experience for me, very nurturing, very beautiful. He was my family, he was really my family, and anyone that he introduced me to that I worked for or designed for, I embellished with the care that I gave to him.

We were soul mates forever, we were. Forever, indeed. His work took him all over the world, and whenever he was out there in different countries, I heard from him. I always managed to send him a beautifully written card through his musical arranger and friend, with the scent of my perfume on it. He said it made him feel as though I was right there with him. I also remember that he loved having a drink of "Courvoisier" cognac every now and then to relax. He would drink it from a wonderful crystal snifter; such an elegant man. He was loved by everybody and adored for his work as a musician, a philanthropist, and anything and everything in-between. What a beautiful man he was.

Besides that, he was the recipient of many Grammy Awards. Many albums that he went on to promote became #1 on the charts in his category of jazz, many times over. I applaud him for all of his courage and his enthusiasm of life, and especially I embrace him for being in my life as well. Love to Jonathan always.

Evan Miro

One day, my neighbor told me about a wonderful person who was working for him doing the painting and the carpentry in his house. The gentleman's name was Evan Miro, and my thoughtful neighbor thought it would be good for me to meet the guy. He said that Evan was Brazilian, very fastidious in his work, and a great person.

"He has very fair prices, and I'm going to give you his number. You call him and tell him I sent you."

When I gave Evan a call he came over, appearing at my front door wearing an entirely white ensemble. White slacks, white shirt, white jacket, and white sneakers—he looked like he was a medical person, a doctor actually, from Brazil. So immaculate and handsome and tall, and he had a smile that just went on for days.

We went through my house as I mentioned the possibility of some jobs I'd been talking about having done for some time: my bedroom, my bathroom, taking wallpaper off, priming, and painting. It was a lot to take in, but Evan seemed to understand just what to do and how long it would take. He gave me an estimate, and I told him his prices were really very fair, and that I'd give him a call as soon as I was ready to start. He took my number and smiled warmly as he said goodbye.

He didn't wait for my call, though. Lo and behold, the next day he called me. "Susan," he said in that fine Brazilian accent, "why don't you meet me for coffee?"

"What time?" I responded.

"About half an hour."

"I'll be there." I suggested that we meet in a very familiar coffee shop in downtown Maryland.

"Yes, thank you. I'm in between jobs right now. Could you meet me? I would appreciate it so much."

When I got to the coffee shop he was seated at a table. He was so thrilled that I'd come to meet him he said, "I really like you." He confided that as soon as I walked in, then added, "I want to know you, Susan."

"But Evan, you do know me," I protested. "And I like you, too. You're very nice."

"Oh no. I really like you." He smiled broadly.

From his warmth and what he said, I could feel my heart racing.

We made arrangements to get together at another time I found more convenient, and he came over some days later. Truthfully, I didn't want to hire him as yet, which might not have been good for his finances, but it was the truth. Sensing he actually did need some work, though, I got him to accompany me to my mother's house to hang up a chandelier in her kitchen. We drove over in my car, and Evan was heating up with every passing mile. Finally, he got so hot and bothered he blurted out his feelings.

"Susan, I want to touch you, may I?"

"What did you have in mind, Evan?"

At that point, his hand caressed my inner thigh and he began to demonstrate exactly what he meant. Evan had the most sensitive fingers and that wonderful craftsman's touch as he slid his hand up and down my inner thigh. I managed to maintain my concentration while driving but it was difficult, because it was obvious to us both how sexually charged our feelings for each other were becoming.

As we arrived at my mother's house it started to rain, making for a very romantic atmosphere. The feeling between us was like a sensual bubble. He seemed disappointed when he told me that he couldn't put up the chandelier after all, being a painter by trade, not an electrician. I didn't mind and my mother didn't, either. The thought was there, she said, and he looked like a nice man. If only she knew where we were headed.

Soon we were on the way back to my house. I had removed my lace panties before we left for the trip back to my house. I leaned over in the car and told him he should touch me once again. He did and it was, wow, fire! So beautiful, wet, juicy. My pussy was delicious once again from his touch, and the thought of everything encouraged more of that to flow. I reached over to him while I was driving. His cock was getting harder and harder inside his pants. It was unbelievable. I thought he was going to just explode and burst out of his pants with his cock throbbing. He moved in his seat just like he was moving on me, but he stayed seated. I thought we were just going to have to pull off the road and complete everything, but we remained patient, and soon were on the approach to my house.

We turned into the driveway and when I mentioned that I had some packages to bring into the house, he offered to help me. As we got out of the car and walked into the garage, I watched him press the button to close the garage door. All of a sudden the garage door was closing.

Evan stood there smiling beautifully at me. He took my hand as I gave it to him willingly and he said, "I would love you to touch me. That would be gorgeous."

"I can do that," I replied, stepping next to him. The packages could wait! I touched him, he touched me. We touched each other in many places. Then he took his cock out of his pants and asked me to stroke him.

I stroked and stroked him! His head went back in total ecstasy as he moaned in guttural delight, and then he came, right on my garage floor! That was something that had certainly never happened before! It was quite the experience, with this quite fun guy. He admitted he'd planned the whole scenario in his mind on the way back to my place.

Before long, I learned how much the cunning gentleman Evan could be. Not long after that, he called me and said he wanted to double-check on the bedroom wallpaper to give me a perfect price on the removal of it. I said okay, and over he came.

I was out in my garden doing some planting, and when I came in I felt I needed to refresh a little bit. I told Evan I was going to go upstairs but first we should have some water with a splash of lemon juice in beautiful cut crystal goblets. He loved that.

Then he said, "Can I come up, too?" I noticed he had already started to follow me. He was following me like a little puppy dog.

I told him, "Sure, you can look at the wallpaper this time."

He was really happy at the positive feeling that I had laid out before him.

I went into the bathroom to wash up a little, and when I came out into the bedroom, Evan was standing there with all his clothes off except for his colorful Brazilian briefs. *Such a beautiful body*, I thought. Oh my god, he was gorgeous, tall, muscular, sensuous and sinewy, so very handsome. His skin was so creamy and delicious looking, and wonderful to touch.

And a ladies kind of man, I told myself. *I'm sure he is, and he's a player. But I'm cool with that, because I knew it from the beginning, right from the get-go.*

The outline of his hard, erect cock inside his underwear moved me to please him and tease him. I could run my fingers along the outline of his cock and trace the length and width of it with my eyes closed. He was so proud of his sexual prowess as he stood before me in a way that said, *Come and get me, I want you!*

And there we were and I was swept up in his arms. He was holding me and touching me and loving me up on top of my bed, generating enough heat it felt like it could strip off the wallpaper. I found myself breathing really heavily now, and with that I asked him to help me take the comforter off the bed. It was amazing. He was so thoughtful and loving and caring and kissing, and what a beautiful time I had with Evan.

Later, I did hire him and found him to be an excellent craftsman, just like my neighbor had said. More importantly, Evan turned out to be a very loving lover, with a Brazilian accent that I continued to think was quite beautiful. I've always been a sucker for accents, but I'm an even bigger sucker for a man whose touch is amazing, whose cock is quite beautiful, who adores me in the way Evan does.

We see each other quite often now, and when we do we have the best time ever. It gets better and better with every visit. I think of him as my very own tropical heat wave, and I've always loved the tropics—especially Brazil.

Jesse Calente

I met a hotter than hot police officer, Mr. Jesse Calente, when he was waiting on horseback, as he was observing the goings-on with traffic activities and such in the downtown area of the big city. I was waiting at the shuttle bus stop for a guest to arrive from Europe at that time. He was perched on his stallion like he would later perch on me, and I couldn't help noticing the beautiful muscles showing in his legs. My eyes devoured the sight, from his boots in the stirrups all the way up to his toned, muscular hips.

I called out, asking if I could come across the street. I'd parked in a no parking zone waiting for my guest, but he didn't seem to notice, or he didn't care.

There was a sizzling undercurrent of sexual tension between us from my first step in his direction. I knew I wanted to have him. You guessed right; eventually, I did.

As I stood next to him while petting his magnificent specimen of a horse, I mentioned I was planning on attending a lecture that evening entitled "How to Flirt."

He responded by saying, "Are you kidding? You don't need to spend money on something like that. You're doing that right now with me." And with that statement, he whipped out his business card and quickly wrote down his personal phone number and said for me to call him.

That night I called, and shortly thereafter we got together. He was an amazingly crazy wild man as a lover! Later, I found out that he was a black belt martial arts instructor. When he was undressed he was gorgeous, all muscles with a beautiful cock that he used ever so well. He knew how to do it well. He was charismatic, a come-hither person, a tease, all the things that women look forward to and get involved with. His policeman's uniform decorated his wonderful body.

I found out later that he was hard to detach from. Jesse's smile was captivating. His full, sensual lips, his Chiclets-like white teeth, always-fresh breath, the whole package.

On warm spring days, many times I would visit the stables to see him and the horses. I loved watching the horses being worked out. Later I found out that he was a big tease and torture kind of guy. He would say, "Perhaps you could use a power nap in the car at this time." He would lie down in my car and pretend to rest. He knew it was killing me, not to immediately jump on his bones, just to sit there and watch him sleep for a minute, or a half hour, or whatever he specified. So I agreed, it killed me, but I did it.

I had my own plans for him at that time. I was needy at this point in my life. I thought that if I said no it would be the end of my relationship with Officer Calente, so that's where I stood at that point in time—not a good place.

Then one day, he invited me to come by at night. I had my own torture in mind. I drove to the stable wearing nothing but my garter belt, thigh high fishnet stockings, and my mink coat that swept the floor. As I walked in, I was carrying a lighted candle. I loved seeing it light up in his eyes. He was still smiling when I put the candle down in a safe place and we disrobed. Amidst the smell of the delicious hay, we had the most amazing time, our lust thrown to the wind of abandonment, moment by moment.

There was nothing short of amazing sex with this sensual, highly charged policeman. Not that we got into handcuffs and such, but one summer night at 2:00 a.m., I heard a knock on my front door. It startled me, since it was a hot summer night and my windows were open. I heard a man's voice call out.

"Susan! Susan! It's Jesse. Please come down and open the door."

Oh, my heart was pounding, since it was the middle of the night. Before I heard his voice, I was going to pick up a phone and call the police. It's a good thing I didn't, since he was a policeman himself. That would have been one for the books.

He used the excuse that he had gone fishing and that he had gotten lost. His creative mind games were off to the races once again. "Yes. I ran out of gas right in

Susan Picosa

your driveway. Imagine the coincidence of something like that."

I realized right then and there that Jesse had been drinking, and it was really something that he had gotten to my house in one piece. He stood there before me and asked if he could come in and take a shower, since he needed one after fishing, as it were.

I was feeling a sense of excitement and creativity, and lied to at the same time. It was a two sides of the coin moment, yes it was.

After he took a shower and returned to his primary role as a sensual, seductive, sly fox of a man, we both fell into bed touching, kissing, holding, licking, sucking and fucking, again and again. It was a marathon of eight hours of non-stop lovemaking. I had to change the sheets three times because they were drenched.

Finally, the morning sunrise began to peek through my curtains, creating streams of sunlight on our now totally loved-up and limp bodies. We had one more moment of, shall we say, a roll in the hay, and then Jesse said that he had an appointment.

I was shocked.

He told me that the mayor was coming to the town and that he had to represent the police force on horseback.

I told him that in no uncertain terms he could stay and be absent from that event. He reluctantly said that he'd go, and after he left, I fell asleep for the rest of the day.

Damn, he wore me out!

An even more amazing experience with Mr. Jesse Calente came one night when we went over to the house of a friend that had a pool. He was out of town. We went straight into the water. The pool had fiber-optic lighting inside that turned the color of the water to red, turquoise, magenta, blue, and green. The temperature outside was about 75°, and I turned the pool temperature up to about 100°. As a result, there was steam just billowing up out of the water, creating a kind of ethereal feeling.

But that was nothing. A summer hailstorm started, showering us with thousands of tiny balls of ice just as we were beginning to have the most amazing sex in the pool. I was sitting on him. His fingers were inside of me. His cock was inside of me. He was licking me.

The contrast of the temperature in the pool and the steam rising out of the water, with the ice cooling us off, was an oh my god moment, the most multifaceted sexual experience that I ever had. It left us breathless and we loved it.

Eduardo

When you embrace love, it can come from the most surprising places.

As a for instance, there was Eduardo, my landscape architect, a gorgeous man with long flowing hair and a tanned, fit body that was a sight to behold, which I certainly did. He was from Argentina. His hands were like the statue of David, long fingers that brought caresses with the sweet palms of his hands, exquisitely tender, yet strongly felt.

Eduardo was exotic and gorgeous and he knew it. He was quite the charismatic lover and he knew that, too. When we made love, it was as though he was designing a spring garden. His embraces and caresses reminded me of how I had seen him labor lovingly over my landscape. It was a touch of this here, a little bit of color there. He lingered, took his time, made me breathe hard, then breathe easy, touching me everywhere and watering me with his loving juices to complete the moment, until everything was just perfect. I was left exhausted.

And then—this still makes me smile—he always ended our lovemaking session with the same simple phrase: "I gotta go."

To where? I never asked! Who knows, to plant another garden or off to another session with the next love struck panting woman waiting passionately for his masterful touch.

I didn't matter to me, because whatever and whenever we did what we did, we always had fun, and Eduardo really adored me. From the scent of lavender roses, to the exotic look of wild orchids, he encouraged me to feel like the most beautiful bouquet of wild flowers, just because.

Ron Shalom

One beautiful sunny day last spring, I looked at my wonderful car with the residue of dust that had accumulated on it through the winter months, and said oh my God it needs to be washed. It *had* to be washed, immediately! I had been very busy and hadn't been to my favorite car wash in a long time. I wondered if I even remembered where it was. But I did, of course, and though I felt a bit neglectful driving in, I was thrilled to watch it coming out so clean.

As I waited for my car to come out the other side, a gentleman who introduced himself as Ron Shalom greeted me. I loved his accent.

"Are you Israeli?" I asked.

He said he was indeed. He was there to make sure my car got the extra treatment I'd paid for, and we struck up a conversation. I told him I had friends that were Israeli, including one woman who was a very close friend of mine.

"Would she go out with me?" he asked, walking around my car inspecting it.

"No, she's married," I replied.

He nodded and continued inspecting my car, then came back around and looked at me intently.

"Is everything okay with my car?"

"Oh sure," he said. "I was just wondering. Will you go out with me?"

I chuckled. I've always had a soft spot for an Israeli accent. I love most accents, actually, because I love people. So I said, okay, and that seemed to make him very happy.

We met in the city another day. We had a cappuccino and we talked and talked for hours. Listening to his Hebrew accent was music to my ears.

Finally, he said, "So Susan, can I come up and see you?"

By then I knew that he lived in another area altogether, a good distance way, but he looked really cute in that carwash outfit with the balloon pants. He had long hair, which I'm a sucker for, was in his early 20s (but over 21, that's for sure) and well, he was just as ripe as a luscious fig, with a smile that could light up the sky at night.

Ron came up to see me at my house, my Ponderosa, and we got to talk for quite a while. He was kosher, so we couldn't eat anything but fruit in my house. I gave him what I had, which was mostly grapes. I fed him the purple orbs; he fed them to me, like we were relaxing in a desert tent, away from the others in the caravan. So romantic.

21

Then we went upstairs to the boudoir and had sex, really great sex. Energetic, enthusiastic, satisfying sex like we were both 20-somethings. Ron was frisky and fun. His body was very slim, quite slender, but that didn't matter because he was in excellent condition and he had a wonderful cock that seemed a bit large for his body, frankly. He knew just what to do, and he kept me cooing when he spoke in Hebrew, which no one had ever done for me. He touched me with the tips of his fingers, caressing my entire body with loving strokes, so as to prepare and stimulate me for what was to come, while I lingered in the moment of pure joy and ecstasy. I was now ready for this young Israeli fox to show me what he's like away from the car wash, in my bed. It was a playful and very sexy time that I had with him.

And then, as we were both relaxing after being totally satisfied, in the middle of everything, he asked me if I heard his cell phone ring. I'd had a wonderful time with him, and by now it was after midnight, but I didn't feel that I wanted him to stay over. Only I didn't hear his phone ring.

"Do you hear that?" he said again. "The phone rang again."

"No, Ron, I didn't hear it."

"Oh yes, it rang. I told my work to call me, if they needed me, I hope you don't mind."

He went over to his phone that was near my full-length mirror, his lean sculptural body a sight to behold once again, and picked it up and pretended to answer it. "I can't believe it!" he said to the phone, feigning a look of exasperation. "You want me to come back and fix the chain in the car wash now?" He paused for effect. "Okay!" he exclaimed, and then hung up.

"What was that?" I asked as he began putting on his pants.

"I'm the only one who knows what to do because my boss knows that I live near the car wash and I have to fix it. Are you upset? Are you mad at me?"

"No, no that's fine," I said. "Don't worry about it." I was having trouble not laughing. This was a move that I'd never experienced before, but I'd heard about in stories. One I thought of writing about, like I am now.

So I drove him to the train and maybe he wasn't really in that big of a hurry after all, because we had one more moment of sex in a Church of Christ parking lot. It was a spontaneous non-planned event, with enough time for us both to have extra special moments to remember, like desert after dinner. Then I dropped him off at the train station and he walked away with a happy Shalom wave.

Ron wanted to get together after that, and I thought about it. He wanted me to come to his place, so I left it with a simple . . . "We'll see."

He wanted to cook me dinner—kosher of course—so one day I might just experience his culinary skills, since I've already given him a four-star rating on his sensual expertise. Meanwhile, he's teaching me Hebrew in our phone conversations, and I love it. He's only teaching me words that are romantic.

Life is what it is and it's always full of surprises. Would Ron and I ever happen again? Probably so. It was certainly another fun adventure.

Elliot Jamal

Mr. Elliot Jamal was a jazz great, a very well known musician. I met him first at a club in a prestigious hotel in the city. He was looking fabulous onstage with his beautiful, midnight blue, satin-lapelled tuxedo and, I soon learned, he thought the same of me as I sat off-stage. He told me that as he looked out across his audience, his thought was, *I have to know her and I will know her*.

There we were after the show, staring at each other, and very soon his thought became reality. We became lovers exceptional. It started out with my going to his place and finding him looking all fabulous in his chocolate brown velour workout ensemble. He had the most gorgeous body, a very contoured musculature. In addition, Elliot was originally from the South, and he had that Southern charm about him.

After we left the music studio in his home, which had a collection of 25 impressive musical instruments, we walked down the hallway to his beautifully appointed bedroom. I couldn't help but notice there was an earthy, very creative aspect to this man with everything in his life. As we entered his sanctuary of delights, he stood there before me with his arms outstretched, waiting to be wrapped around me. I easily allowed myself to be enveloped.

Elliot was quite a lover. He touched me like he played his instrument. The thought of it even now makes me hot and wet. Elliot Jamal stroked my body like he stroked his instrument, throwing all my inhibitions to the side. When he loved me up, it was as though he was playing music for me, from rhythmical passionate pulsating beats to a place that he took me to that made all my warm juices spill out, like real sweet music. He always had an intoxicating smile, especially when he knew that he had accomplished every erotic moment to its fulfillment.

His body was so beautiful, and he would bring me to climax so easily, his touch creating intoxicating magical sensations. His brown skin magnificence was so wonderful inside of me, filling me up because he was so velvety to touch and so very well endowed. Oh yes, the boy was well endowed.

As he continued to nibble on my earlobes and whispered soft, sexy thoughts of encouragement to let me know everything he was going to do to me in the next few minutes, oh my, oh my, how wet and excited I became.

There was a method to this man's madness for sure. I began to undress this beautiful specimen of a man, taking my sweet time, observing every delicious inch of his body.

As I continued, he reached down and began unbuttoning my blouse, undid my bra, and then I let him take my skirt off and then my lace panties.

There we stood, completely naked before each other, thoughts running wild with expectations of what was going to be happening.

He reached out and took my hand and led me to his wonderful king-sized bed. I willingly laid myself down on his white Egyptian cotton sheets, so cool to the touch against my warm body.

At that moment, I remembered that in my handbag I had a beautiful, hand-painted silk scarf. Without interrupting the moment, I reached across the bed, took out the scarf, and draped it over his lampshade. We both whispered thoughts of how beautifully the colors reflected into the room and enhanced the already magical moment.

Elliot began stroking me with rhythmically fine-tuned magical fingers in the way that he played his instruments. He caressed and nibbled on every inch of my body with his soft tongue, exploring crevices with sweet licking sounds. How wet I become as I caressed his beautiful cock with strokes that encouraged it to become so hard and throbbing with thick creamy juices. I wrapped my mouth around his warm cock, my lips encircling it totally. As it slowly moved in and out, becoming harder with every second, until he couldn't stand it any longer, he begged me to let him enter my temple of paradise, his long fingers opening the lips of my warm pussy, and now I was ready to receive him. Oh how wonderful he felt.

Susan Picosa

As he entered me, I felt the sensation of exquisite interior caresses from his beautiful cock, stroking him lovingly as the walls of my pussy squeezed him tightly. The heat of the moment left us breathless on drenched cotton sheets and let us know that we would be returning to that place of sensual delights soon again.

Of course, we have, and we always will.

Norman McKnight

One little fun caper was with Mr. Norman McKnight, a famous DJ, a model, an actor, and above all quite the sexy guy.

Oh yes, he is the latter, and always will be.

We had spent some time together, laughing, talking a lot, and finally one evening he came over to my house, the first time he had been here. Norman was visiting his family, who live near me, but he lived quite a distance away.

During our time together, I mentioned something I thought he'd like. I was just feeling out the potential of possibilities of a later sexual moment with him, so to speak. "Did I tell you that I have some really hot and naughty porn tapes?"

Norman looked at me quizzically, tilting his head to the side, and then a big smile appeared on his lips. "Oh? No, you didn't."

"Well, would you like to see them?" It was an aha, a little come-on, come-hither moment, that's all. He was a gorgeous model; did I have a chance? Would this well known DJ, this quite the famous guy who could be with anyone he wanted because he was that attractive, give me even a passing thought about something like that?

I guess he did. There we were, upstairs in my bedroom, sitting on the edge of my bed, hands behind us on the bedspread, watching this red hot, steamy, sizzling, no holds barred videotape, and wouldn't you know, all of a sudden we were making out like crazy.

We fell back on the bed and I discovered his body was just as wonderful as I imagined it might be under his clothes. He was brown skinned with a body that went on for days. His touches were methodically placed, so as to arouse every possible sensual sensation in my body. He was capable of extracting ribbons of white creamy juices from me, by having me cum in his hand as he touched me with his sensitive fingers, and at the same time licking me with his luscious tongue. His lovemaking was exquisite and he held nothing back. Totally satisfied and exhausted, we stopped to look at each other somewhat shocked that we had gone to that place, but didn't regret a minute of it. Wow, was that a spontaneous minute, or what?! Truly amazing!

It was just one of those rare gifts. We had a great time and stayed good friends. We don't see each other that often, and we haven't gone there again, but what a memory. What a wonderful, memorable moment that was. Norman, baby, you're HOT! Like the old song said, Oh What A Night!

Explorations

One benefit of the sexual transformation in my life was that I was willing to explore just about anything, to a degree, whether it be in conversation or actual exploration. I was continually surprised at myself, considering what I'd been denied all the years of my marriage, and some times I felt like my horizons were continuing to expand, experiencing each new moment with curiosity. Those new feelings of maturity led me to explore the more X-rated side of life.

One day I decided to go into the city and visit an X-rated shop that had CDs and videos. This was before DVDs, and I was used to videos—VHS.

I told the gentleman at the counter that I was doing a project on masturbation.

"Lady, we don't have videos really any more. We have some CDs." Then he yells out: "Masturbation CDs, Aisle #5! Masturbation CDs, Aisle #5!"

Everybody was looking at me, standing there like a deer in the headlights. Or a stripper naked for the first time onstage. Then near me, one guy—I'd quickly noticed they had a lot of skeevy-looking people there—said to me: "You have beautiful hair, lady. Oh, it looks so pretty."

I was getting pretty freaked out. Then the clerk said: "Lady, we don't have videos, we have CDs, so if you want you can go down the street and get another video or something. You ask there." He handed me a business card for the other porn shop. Obviously, they helped each other do business.

So down the street I went, and used the same approach there. "Hi. I'm working on a project for masturbation. I need a video."

"Okay!" This time it was a guy from—I believe—Russia. "We have some videos. Masturbation videos, Aisle #7!" with an accent very heavy, you could hardly understand him. Maybe he was from one of the "Stans" like Kazakhstan?

I was freaked out but I wasn't going to leave empty-handed. I found a couple of videos and a couple of masturbation CDs, and I left.

As I was going out the door I thought, this is so weird, the way it's announced in the shops is amazing, but I'm a big girl. I can go and do these things now, but did it have to be such a big announcement? After the second shop, I half-expected a hidden camera crew to pop out of a back room and tell me I was on network TV, live!

If that wasn't embarrassing enough, there was the blue vibrator. I decided to go visit a little sex shop in my area. I'd found out from a girlfriend that they had CDs, videos, vibrators, sexy lingerie, as well as anything and everything that was necessary for those steamy, X-rated experience moments.

Well, as soon as I walked in this cobalt blue vibrator caught my eye. I picked it up and began to admire it, and the woman who owned the shop began to explain its many benefits. Thankfully, she was thoughtful in the way she described everything.

"It touches the G-spot," she said matter-of-factly. "It touches the clitoris, and it just moves and grooves and does all these things magical."

So I took it home and I tried it and even though I knew what the buttons did, I said to myself, this is not for me. It was too much of a full mechanical thing with too many buttons to push and rotating things and damn, what were they thinking? I went downstairs, threw it in the garbage, closed the pail, and that was it.

Only it wasn't. About half an hour later I noticed some sounds coming from the garage and I went to investigate. The garage pail was vibrating and moving along the floor. It was definitely a turn-off and not a turn-on.

I opened the garage pail and removed the blue toy. I removed the batteries immediately and it stopped doing its thing. I threw the vibrator back in the garbage pail and closed the lid tightly. No more rockin' 'n rollin' for me, unless I'm doing it for myself! Peace at last.

Then halfway up the stairs I wondered if the garbage man was going to notice it in there. Maybe he would, maybe he wouldn't, I decided. Maybe if he did it would be a good thing for him, who knows. As for me, from that point on I wanted the real thing!

That wasn't my last adventure with the more vocal side of sex. When my business was a little slow, I was talking with a knowledgeable friend (that's as much as I'll say about it) and was told that I could become a phone sex operator and make between $1,000 and $10,000 a week if I did 24/7 daily postings of listings, recordings, greetings, and ads, and then went to chat rooms as well. It sounded like a lot of work, but a lot more money, considering that I would be sitting around just talking on the phone.

At that time I didn't know all the specifics but I was ready to commit. I had the phone company install a second line for my home, a private line, and I received an 800 number from a company. After that I went to town, dived into the business.

And then, I waited. I turned all the TVs off at night, I put some lighted candles around for atmosphere, turned out all the other lights, and sat patiently, expecting that the phone would light up and ring.

I had some very steamy greetings posted on my phone sex operator line. I posted ads that were X-rated hot and changed them pretty regularly. I was plugged into Brazil, Argentina, France, Israel, Italy, and locally to different states as well as major cities like New Orleans, and New York City. I figured I'd done everything right.

Nothing happened. Absolutely nothing.

I sat there in the dark watching my candles burn down for a few days. I would be available from 6:00 until 10:00 at night. At first I'd kept earlier hours, but then I reasoned that from 5:00 p.m. to 7:00 p.m., people (married men) would have to disappear into the bathroom to answer my ad on their cell phone and get off that way. Finally, I admitted that I would have to adjust my hours to reach the main body of men. So I changed to the later hours, but still nothing happened.

Then my friend reminded me to go into a chat room, get on chat lines, so I did that. I chose the groups of people that I wanted to connect with: single men, bisexual men, men into dominatrixes, married men, I didn't care. The ages I focused on were from 30 to 50.

Maybe that would fix it. I was a good actress; I could do anything!

Finally, when I posted the greeting in the chat places, the response was unbelievable. A ton of calls came in. The catch was, nobody wanted to pay the $3.99. They wanted to just chat on the chat line and get off while they were communicating to me that way.

"That's it!" I yelled to the walls the last night of my experiment. "I'm not doing this any more, it's not my thing!"

I had the phone disconnected. I called the person that originally set me up with the 800 number and asked for a refund. I got a partial refund for both the phone and the 800 line. I was so relieved. All that, I thought, just to earn a couple of extra dollars. Even if I'd been able to earn $1,000 to $10,000 a week, I realized the whole thing just wasn't my style. That's when I decided to write my book. I decided it would to be the thing that really did it for me. Let me know what you think!

Lester Lauder

I've never met a black man with a small cock. That's what "they" say and it seems like a cliché, but you know what? It's true, for me, anyway. Take, for example, Lester Lauder, whom I met when he responded to a personal ad. Lester was a handsome Jamaican gentleman with a lot of charm. Here's how it all began.

"You're just what I've been looking for my whole life," he said, widely grinning at me.

"Your whole life of like, 35 years? Or maybe 30 years?" I chuckled; I was a little older than that at the time.

I'd been staring at him because he was so flawlessly gorgeous. His long legs, so beautifully muscular, supported a 6'5" body, and were the perfect match to his gorgeous hands, which were reaching over toward me, as we sat at the restaurant table.

"I have really have been looking for you forever," he repeated. "Susan, you're like the perfect person for me!"

I admit it; I melted right then and there, not really knowing him. I was swept up in the moment, which turned out to be a big, big mistake.

I was getting very clear signals as to the smooth-talking player that I was going to get involved with, partially at least, because he was so sensual and so sexy, but it took time before we actually got together. When that happened, he came over and demonstrated that he was an amazing lover who had fine-tuned his craft like to a point where there was nothing missing, nothing at all except a conscience.

As we entered my bedroom, I could see his pants becoming noticeably tighter in the crotch area, with a bulge that was hard to miss, and harder not to touch. I unzipped his pants, wanting to see the whole package of what awaited me, and the most incredible moment was on view for me to participate in. Not only did his cock unfurl the likes of which I'd never seen, but he tucked it downward inside his briefs, since he was too big to just let it rest like the average man's penis. He stroked it with pride in front of me, so that I could witness the length and circumference of it. He could make it dance for me. This was a sexual sight to behold.

This man had a well-crafted sex machine way about him. Being teased by him in order to be turned on even more was his M.O. He would tease and torture me until I couldn't stand one more minute of not having him, and it worked. I wanted him NOW!

Lester took his sweet time opening up the foil wrapper of the magnum condom he'd brought along. It was as though he was removing the wrapper from a delicious chocolate candy. His way of ever so carefully using his long fingers and gorgeous hands to roll the condom down his gorgeous cock was like a ritual in itself. I felt the care he took with this preparation would continue with the care he would take with me, and I was right.

He entered me with the same gentle, careful not to hurt way. As his cock filled me up with amazing warmth, he continued touching me all over with his fingers, while whispering things in my ear that made me revel in every moment of his sexual dialogue. Lester turned me on in ways that were very hard to compare to anyone else. He brought me to a climax that few ever gave me. I was drenched and dripping in delight with wetness that tasted sweet and creamy. Ours was a sexual parfait.

As the evening went on he would continue to convince me that I was a sexual feast.

"Look at that!" he would say. He would point to my breasts with his palms extended, as I stood before him naked. "Just look at that!"

His "look at that" just melted me one more time. It was captivating for me because I was vulnerable at that time. I loved it, and I still have fond memories of it, but boy was I needy then. What I didn't realize was that it was all a ritual Lester had used repeatedly.

But we live and learn. The main thing was that, other than his being an amazing lover, Lester promised things and never delivered. When he would leave after making love to me, he might say, I'll call you later, and a week went by before "later" turned into "when." Any time I was left hanging, it was always disappointing to me, and after enough of those dashed expectations, I finally reached the last straw.

"We're going to have a great Christmas," he told me one year. "You're going to have a beautiful little tree and you'll celebrate. You're going to love it. I'm going to make you so happy!"

So I went out shopping with him, we picked out a nice little tree, I decorated it a little bit, and he was going to come over and finish helping me with the decorating.

And you know what? I know you know what happened. Nothing happened! He never showed up, ever. Lester was a real smooth talker and he was a not-so-smooth player.

Eventually, I realized I'd had the best of him, in the times we were together, and that was the end of him for me. Yes, it was. Sex is something I love, but deception is not.

Ted Gotto

Another gentleman that I met through the Internet personal ads was a Mr. Ted Gotto. He was very young. When I went to meet him, he was waiting for me and sitting on the side of a street in a small town in Rhode Island. He was wearing his backpack and at first I wondered if he was in college. It turned out he was only 25, and there I was in my late 40s! When we met we both looked a bit surprised. I found out that by the sound of my voice on the phone, Ted thought I was much younger, around his age. He mentioned to me that had recently come to this country from Cape Verde.

As we were having coffee, though, he suggested we could be friends. He didn't know if it would go any further.

That's how what turned into a relationship lasting 15 years started out, in a friendly way but one that didn't take long to turn sexual.

Ted had a passion for being observed doing things. He was a passionate narcissist, a person very self-involved, and I understood and respected that. I admired that he was also a creative person, which I really found out when we went to bed. He was a very attentive lover to me, very attentive, knew how to touch me, be inside of me, how to nuzzle me, how to be attentive to my breasts and my legs, and he loved to let me dance for him, especially to my Latin rhythms.

He was a person very much appreciative of me in every way, but the personal limitations of being a narcissist finally made our relationship cross over to a place that I couldn't take any more. But later on that.

I loved watching him do his photography and his artwork, too. I am an artist, so the appreciation of our creative thoughts encouraged a mutual playground for both of us. He would always come to my gallery openings, in whatever city they were in, and let me know how much he loved my art. My work has the passion that reflects itself in every area of my life. He was a very multifaceted artist as well. I found him to be very artistic in everything he approached, including making love to me! Ted wore interesting bracelets, silver bangles that were like melodic wind chimes making all these beautiful sounds. When he caressed me, his fingers inside of me exploring my love region, he paid close attention to my ever-increasing passion and, knowing when I was going to reach a climax, his touch became more in tune with my breathing, and the bracelets echoed the rhythm like passionate musical sounds on his arm.

That was so memorable for me, so gorgeous. And then there was his hair, long and flowing, down to his waist. He'd take out the clip and let it drape freely over his shoulders and face, like a beautiful guru when he made love to me. His Portuguese words that expressed his passion in the moment, his positioning of me in various ways that gave us both the deepest and most generous feelings in our lovemaking, were all things that he prided himself on, and that we both enjoyed to the fullest. He was a very knowing man in the area of exceptional lovemaking. Wasn't I the lucky one?! I'll give him a five star rating on that!

When we first met, Ted was living at his mother's house, way up in Rhode Island. He invited me over, and we were only there a short time when he announced his desire to make love to me, since his mother wasn't home.

I was glad she wasn't, because she might have learned just how amazingly creative her son could be. I was in his bedroom beginning to take my clothes off when he came in carrying a full-length mirror, which he set against the wall near the bed.

His bedroom was plain and simple, just the normal amount of furniture, with a mirror on the wall, but it wasn't in the position Ted wanted. He placed the tall mirror, being the narcissist that he was, in a position so that he could he could turn and observe himself while making love to me, positioning me every way possible to achieve the very heightened climactic moment that we both were there for. Oh yes, yes, we sure did. And to top things off he was able to capture every one of his poses in the mirror. You go, boy!

Oh, the things I'd failed to learn at his age! It was my first experience of something like that but I thought it was cool.

Susan Picosa

So many wonderful things happened over the time Ted and I knew and loved each other, and they never failed to be interesting. He made me a cougar when I wasn't even trying to be one, and whenever I think of him, I still feel like purring with delight. Meow.

Naughty Robert

Our first meeting was supposed to be a surprise at a very elegant, high-end restaurant downtown Boston, where we were supposed to have our first date. Naughty Robert was a cunning Scottish Caribbean man, a sly fox with women, who had a way with words for everyone, including me. He wanted me to meet him at a well-patronized shopping center, and then he would drive me to the restaurant after I parked my car, in order to surprise me as far as the restaurant that he was taking me to.

I called to tell him that I had arrived, and Robert suggested that I flirt with all the security guards until he picked me up, and tell him all about it in detail later. That was a very voyeuristic comment, and the way that things started out were not great. If voyeuristic didn't say it all, what else did? He kept me waiting at the mall for about one hour, and said that he was stuck in traffic, probably a non-truth.

When I first met him at a speed-dating event, he had come across as humble, thoughtful, and kind of shy. Actually, I first thought he was a little needy, but Robert was impressive, very bright, an architect and a pilot as well. On top of that, he was a very, very kinky lover whom I soon learned had bisexual women in his life. Robert liked all that kind of stuff because he was a total voyeur, if you know what I mean. He liked to watch. Everything.

It didn't take me long to realize when we first arrived at the restaurant that I was not the first woman he'd taken to this beautiful place. He knew everybody. They came out to greet him. The chefs came out as well. I was one among many, but that didn't matter. It was the first place that we went to, and he knew the place extremely well, if you know what I mean. I just wanted to continue getting to know him, although his true colors started showing immediately.

He told me that he really liked me and that things were going to become absolutely wonderful between us. He wanted to take it nice and slow. Slow? *Molasses* was the operative word here.

But there was something great about being with him. When our evening ended, I was dancing outside of my car at twelve midnight. I had opened all of the windows of my car and cranked up the volume on the stereo, pressed play, and the Latin sounds of Marc Anthony's "Si Tu No Te Fueras" were resonating throughout the shopping center parking lot. There were hardly any other cars left. Robert was watching me dance, and I really turned it out and turned him on. The security guard passed by several times but just kept going, probably thinking we were out of our minds. I was feeling extremely free and happy at that moment, and I was able to express it in my dancing for him.

We'd been listening to Latin music and I felt very happy to have met this man. I still had a lot to learn about him. The way I thought he was, he wasn't at all. He had my attention, though. Robert was a very

46

beautiful specimen of a dark-skinned man who was able to converse with anyone, on any subject with ease. That was part of his appeal for me.

After I made a certain comment, he said to me, "Size matters."

I said, "No it doesn't, size doesn't matter."

He said, "Absolutely, it does."

I soon learned he wouldn't say that if he weren't well endowed. He was all that, and more.

He was also all over me, literally! The first night we got together, he would hold me after we made love, and every time I turned away he would pull me close and hold me again.

Every time I shifted in bed, he was wrapped around me. He loved me up beautifully, several times throughout the night. He loved sucking on my breasts, caressing them, and was quite the adventurer, exploring every inch of my body.

In the morning at 5:00 a.m. he had to pilot a charter flight for a charter group, so I got up, and lovingly prepared tea and crumpets for us. Then, after some don't forget me touches and wet kisses, off he went. He knew how to work it! It's funny, his flight bag left such an impression on my carpet that when he took it with him, four black dots from the wheels remained, and I couldn't get them out, so it's a constant reminder that Mr. Naughty Robert was here.

The next experience with Mr. Naughty was in a pool owned by his friend, and the voyeur appeared once again.

"Why don't we see about contacting my friend who owns the house?" he mentioned with a sly grin.

"Why?" I asked. "What did you have in mind?"

"Well, he likes to have fun. I was thinking he could come out and watch us have sex and jerk off in the bushes. Wouldn't that be wild?"

That's the kind of guy he was. We didn't do that, of course, but he would have loved it. He's a voyeur, freaky, but he comes across as a very proper person with that Scottish accent and his impressive credentials as an architect with a pilot's license.

We're friends to this day, just friends, by my choice of course. I don't judge what he likes; it's his life, but I sure learned some lessons from this man.

D'Andre Moses

Here is Mr. D'Andre Moses—a master pianist, a master vocalist, a genius altogether. D'Andre is another jazz legend who got to know me, little by little.

One night, I was attending a performance of his in a club that many jazz greats frequent. After he played this song that I was crazy about, I went up to him and I told him how I felt about it.

"I'm just enamored with everything that you've done," I said. "You're just a beautiful man."

He looked over at me and smiled. I wasn't sure how he was going to react. Then he glanced down at my hand and began to admire a beautiful ring that I had designed. Slowly, he reached down and lifted my fingers closer, to get a better look.

"Why, that's just amazing," he said. "Thank you for the compliment about the music, but I must know where you got this ring!"

"It's a black opal," I explained. "It's in its matrix. It's the shape of an egg, which you can see, the size of a small hummingbird egg to be exact."

He kept holding my hand, admiring the ring and smiling at me with his eyes.

Susan Picosa

"I want one of those!" he exclaimed. "Do you by any chance have another?"

"No, but we can be friends, and maybe I can come up with something for you?"

He laughed, kissed my ring, and gave me back my hand. "You strike a hard bargain, you gorgeous thing, you. Tell you what. I'm going to invite you to an amazing recording session. It's a first for this up and coming artist that I recently discovered, and the person in question, that you are going to hear and witness, is going to be a major star. Can you dig that?"

That was many years ago and I did attend the recording session. The lady who was there at the piano when I walked into the studio, had a big Afro and dark shades and looked like she was born to be a star. As she sat at the piano and accompanied her own vocals, she transformed the studio into such a magical place, the likes of which I'd never heard. She just performed in a way that took your breath away, and it was absolutely exceptional. She has since become an extremely famous performer.

I watched as they went through the first song, and then went for another take. When the third one started up, I realized that I needed to make a phone call, so I asked where I could find the phone booth. That's how people made calls in those days; all the studios had phone booths. There were no cell phones or anything like them.

So off I went off down a hall, digging in my purse for coins, and as I reached the phone booth I turned and saw, right behind me, putting his hand on my shoulder, kissing my neck, none other than Mr. D'Andre Moses.

Oh my, oh my! He got the point that I wasn't really there to be hugged up and kissed on, as I told him, "I'll see you back in the studio. That's what I came for and that's what I'll listen to."

"Of course, of course," he said. He walked away like a puppy with his tail between his legs, but we made up for it later on, so to speak.

D'Andre and I became best, best of friends. I continued attending his performances and designing beautiful dashikis for this extra special genius of a man. He was so fine, and appreciated everything I did. I added touches of beautiful crystals to his sleeves so that when he played and he faced the audience on one side, it was adorned with beautiful crystals in all different colors.

Dashikis were his thing, and silk scarves that he draped over the microphones some times when he was performing. He would say, "I have my designer right here in the house, stand up and take a bow."

And I did. He always wears things well, and never fails to thank me royally.

One evening, he called and offered me this wonderful opportunity to sit opposite him in a very prestigious club in his dressing room where only the elite could come in and visit with him, after his performance.

He said, "How about this one?"

"I'm ready to hear your request, Mr. Fabulous."

"Why don't you come in to the club without panties, just panty-less, and sit directly across from me in my dressing room?"

I said, "Wow, this is going to be a first, but an amazing experience, so why not? I'm young, fabulous, pretty, and I do have dancer's legs, so why not show them off. If I do that, then what?"

He laid out the plan as follows. "When I look over at you and nod, you open your legs, just ever so slightly, just enough so that I can take a peek at your pussy, just a little peek, please baby. 'It will be our very own little secret, and no one will know what we're up to.

"Aw, baby. That will be amazing for me," he said, and you'll just love my little game as well.

I told him goodbye and hung up, laughing. D'Andre would be playing well that night, I knew it.

So that evening, after his performance, we went upstairs to his dressing room suite where his guests were waiting to congratulate him on everything. As they began to come in and enthuse about his performance, giving him hugs and kisses, I made sure that I was seated directly across from him before his guests were allowed to come through the door. I sat poised and ready, with my legs just slightly opening every time he would nod. He was so free and creative; the word that best describes him at times like those is "freaky." He absolutely loved it, and occasionally made little guttural noises that caused his friends to wonder what was going on. Only he and I knew he could see just a little bit of my pussy after every nod, and that he was in seventh heaven with everything that I was doing.

One other incident that was amazing was on a boat cruise we took around an island. I wore one of my best designs, a raw silk, white dress hand-painted with gorgeous color confetti dots reflecting in the sunset, beautiful and flowing, with a matching caftan over it, a coat that just sort of billowed out and fluttered in the wind. I was standing on deck, my hair blowing in the wind, when D'Andre came up behind me. He was the performer on the boat that night with his band, and taking his break. He just enveloped me with his arms around me, pressing against me, discovering my breasts and all the contours of my body with both hands. His fingers searched out my every crevice, as he took me to another place of beautiful.

"You are wetter than the river we're riding on," he told me, his mouth nuzzled against my neck. Oh my, how the wind was blowing, and the spray of the water on us was amazing. The people that had attended the performance of Mr. D'Andre Moses and his band were just walking around the deck looking at the water, talking about the performance. We were in our own

Susan Picosa

world, loving it up, touching, exploring, and we took full advantage of every intimate moment, and they were clueless, just clueless. What a caper that was.

Ahh. It takes my breath away to recall that one. D'Andre, you make beautiful music with me.

Father Michael Garrick

Believe it or not, there was a man of the cloth, a priest, who added wonderfully to my experiences in life. His name was Father Michael Garrick and he was something else. When I first met him, I was attending a performance of some musicians, one of whom I knew very well, at the Father's church. It was a Christian music program and I saw Michael the moment I walked down the aisle. There he sat, up there on the dais, looking all kinds of fabulous.

Father Garrick was a brown skin gentleman, 6'7" or 6'8" in stature, and I could tell he was having a great time, just moving and grooving to the music in his beautiful African garb.

"Wow," I said to a woman sitting next to me. "Who is that marvelous man up there?"

She told me, chuckling, and then, as if she knew what was on my mind, she added, "Oh yes, I know exactly you mean, sister."

Later, when I went backstage to congratulate my friends on their performance, Father Garrick was in the crowd. As soon as I paid my compliments, the object of my earlier affection turned to me and said, "And who might you be, you pretty little thing?"

Was what I thought was happening really going on? "Well, I'm a designer," I said. I waved my hand at my musician friends. "I work with these people and I came to support them."

"Maybe you can design some vestments for me," he said. "Any chance of that?"

"Of course there is!" My breath was taken away at that moment as I looked into his admiring eyes. He gave me his card, I gave him mine, and we continued to speak, about many things. He told me how wonderful I was, and I told him how magnificent he was. We talked about a time to possibly get together.

"The thing is," he said, "I never get away! I'm always on call, 24 hours a day, as the priest at the parish." He was shaking his head, looking a bit dejected.

"Maybe someday we can just find some time to go out for a little bite to eat or something, and talk about your vestments? I'm patient."

He smiled. "How about this? Why don't you come to the rectory one day?"

We promised to work out a date. The next day I talked to my musician friend and learned that the Father was a very well-known man who had been written up in the newspapers for changing things in communities in a very positive way. I felt honored to have met him. I later found out that Father Garrick was always selected each year to be a speaker on diversity at the Roundtable, at a very prestigious university. And to sing his praises a little more, he had been responsible for building schools in deprived areas where children had to end their studies after the sixth grade, so that they could go out to work and help support their family.

I felt honored to have met him. The more I found out about him, the more my breath was taken away. Then one day he called and explained to me that when he could get away, he would go to his sister's house for quiet moments, just to watch the flowers grow, and spend quiet time in the gardens, just to walk around away in a peaceful place away from his parish. He was going to be there the next day. Maybe I could join him and talk about my art and other things?

So I did go there with the intention of designing some exquisite artwork for him, and took along some of my paintings to generate some ideas. As I walked toward his sister's garden to present my work, there I saw him, at the top of a landing on the steps, in all of his magnificence once again. He grinned when he saw me and beckoned me to come up to the top of the stairs. When I arrived, he had his arms outstretched. He swept me up the biggest hug and then, to my delighted surprise, planted a kiss right on my lips!

Can you believe that? Ahh, I thought, this is going to be a story for the books. It was bigger than any consideration either of us had to the otherwise. We were enraptured with each other, just two human beings having met in a unique way and feeling the way we did as though nothing else in the world mattered.

I feel that, that day, we became very best friends, forever for life. To this day, he is a soul mate of mine forever, and I of his forever. We are always in touch.

And naturally, there is more to the story.

One night, he did come over and stay with me, on the way home from his sister's house. It was the unthinkable to some, but it was wonderful for us.

We didn't have actual sex. We slept together in the bed and caressed and touched. I loved him, and wanted to share the real essence of the word "intimate" with him, and all things considered, that was better than sex.

How? Just better, if you can understand that one.

Before going to sleep we watched a program called "The Naked News" on the computer, him in his black watch plaid shorts and me in my silk nightgown. We laughed till tears were rolling down our cheeks.

The next morning, we went downstairs and I made beautiful breakfast for the both of us, pecan pancakes dripping with warm butter, fresh fruit compote, fresh coffee with cream and after all was said and done, then I sent him on his way. So there you have it. I've either plunged to new depths, or risen to new heights. It's all in the eyes of the reader.

And that was it. Ever since we've been very good friends, and best soul mates now for life. It feels like such a blessing. He's heaven-sent to all that have been blessed to know him. Amen.

Alexis

Alexis was my partner in crime for quite some time. We met many years, many, many moons ago. I answered his personal ad and agreed to meet him at a restaurant. When he saw me, he told me later, he thought I was a college student. I was in my 40s and he was 20-something, very smart, very handsome, a Denzel Washington as a young man look-alike.

When I told him my age, he said he didn't think it was going to work. I agreed we could be just friends and see what happened from there.

I'd also been through what developed after that! Knowing the potential, I left it as-is. Little by little (and little did I know it would), that friendship developed into something much more steamy.

Alexis had a body that was, oh my goodness, breathtaking. Breathtaking, I say! He was tall, maybe 6'5", contoured like a sculpture, and his cock was really amazing. Truly amazing.

We got together from time to time, but neither of us had the idea of being exclusive with each other. Whenever he got involved with someone that was more age appropriate, we would take a time out. Other times, he would be going with someone who wanted to know who he slept with. He would explain that he had to call and get clearance before he left to come and see me.

You know, I learned to take it for what it was, because I definitely enjoyed him a lot.

One experience that stands out I call the eye contact moment.

Oh my goodness. What happened was, we always had safe sex. I always did that with all the men I was involved with, always. So we decided this time if he didn't use a condom he could just be between my breasts with his cock, and it was very ample, so there was no problem there. I put lotion between my breasts, on my breasts, everything to make things really silky and delicious, enjoying every moment as I did watching him. And he loved it, just loved it. But what happened is when he ejaculated, the cum went right, like a dart, like a bullet right into my eye, and I thought I'm blind, I'm blind, that's it, hang up the rock 'n roll shoes. He was so upset and apologetic.

I had to call my ophthalmologist. It was the middle of the night and I had to tell him exactly what happened! He had a big laugh about that one. "Just keep it closed as much as you can," he told me, "but bathe it with ophthalmic saline solution and you'll be fine."

So we did continue that kind of feature every now and then but at a point in time we decided we were going to have a washcloth and he would tell me exactly when the moment of ejaculation would occur and I would block it with the washcloth. And that was it. A good time was had by all after that, with the potential of new and exciting creative moments to come.

Jullian Smith

I met a beautiful police officer, Mr. Jullian Smith, at the clothing optional beach. He was in the gay section by accident; he didn't know the beach that well. So there he was and wouldn't you know it? He was looking at me. I spotted him as I was taking a walk along the beach.

"Am I in the wrong section?" he asked. He came closer to me.

"Yes you are," I said. "But from the looks of things, you should be just fine."

It wasn't hard to become talkative from there. We walked around for about an hour, talking about everything, and he said he'd like to call me. I had no objection at all. Jullian was exquisite, with light brown caramel-colored skin. A nice touch to this handsome specimen was his little dreadlocks. It wasn't something I expected on a police officer, but he was a free spirit. At the same time, he was a bit shy, like a young teenage boy. He was just beautiful as a person, and I was magnetically drawn to him.

Finally, he came over to my home one night and brought along some beautiful plates of shellfish from his favorite seafood place in another city. There before me were platters of lobster, shrimp, and clams on the half shell on ice with beautifully cut lemon wedges.

Also a huge bucket of mussels impeccably prepared, and cooked in a sauce of white wine, olive oil, garlic, and lemon juice. Oh yes, there was a method to his choice of shellfish, two dozen oysters on the half shell as well. I know those babies are an aphrodisiac, so a good time would be had by all very shortly. Good thinking, Mr. Smith. An amazing feast to enjoy before the moments that awaited us. As time went by, I would learn he would continually think of wonderful and creative things like that to do.

Jullian was a state trooper. He was strong, handsome, and quite the gentle lover—not something I would naturally expect of a police officer. He had come to me on a very beautiful summer day when sunshine caressed us like a warm smile, and each moment we had together seemed to have that same feeling of perfect heat. We swam nude in a nearby crystal clear lake that had a very private cove, and took full advantage of the moment, making love several times with sounds that inspired the birds to sing to us, as we devoured each other with erotic sexual passion. His tongue, his lips, his cock, his freckles, all merged with me in that heated moment. Yes, I did say his freckles. They seemed to dance on his face for me, when the sunlight touched them.

He told me that he loved my breasts, my nipples, and my pussy. Everything about me, he said, felt so delicious. I felt protected and taken care of at the same time, and the more Jullian complimented me, the more he made me understand that he really did feel what he was telling me. I'd never felt so admired.

Jullian visited me several times during that summer. Every time, we got more and more into each other and never ceased to love it.

And then something happened that really touched me. He got into a really bad accident while doing his duty as a state trooper out on the highway and hurt his knee so badly he had to retire from being a trooper.

Thankfully, the rehabilitation made him seem good as new to me, and he didn't let the setback get to him. He decided to change his profession and become a registered nurse, which I felt was an excellent profession for him, better than being a trooper, because Jullian was such a very caring and nurturing man.

Then one morning he called me. I was watching television while we talked, but on a different station than the one he'd been watching. The date was September 11th.

"Put it on the news!" he yelled.

I changed the channel right away, just as Jullian was yelling on the other end. He'd seen the jet plane hit the first tower of the World Trade Center. We hardly said anything to each other—nothing I remember, anyway—as we watched the rest of the awful events play out.

That day bonded us forever. Like so many other millions of people, that was something that I'll never forget, ever. And because Jullian and I watched that experience together, yet apart, at the same time, this sad, very tragic day made me feel ever so closer to him.

Life can be so multifaceted at times.

Charles Bernal

There was a Brazilian gentleman by the name of Charles Bernal who came to me through a friend of mine. I was told he had the most exquisite gemstones from Brazil that one could ever imagine. I really thought at that moment, *I need to take a look at those.*

I was given his phone number, and when I called him, he came over and when he stood before me there was an innocence about him, a smile that lit up the room, as well as a gentle quality about his conversation with me. He had the most exquisite accent from Brazil, and I do love accents as I've said before.

He opened his portfolio and in a few quick, expert movements, he displayed his crystals, all of his gemstones, on my dining room table. He took the jewels out of their packages and laid them out as though he was performing at a royal court, and my friend was exactly right when he described them as exquisite. They were like paradise on my dining room table, shining in the afternoon sunlight filtering through the curtains. I thought, *What a beautiful experience this is going to be!*

As I looked at these amazing crystals and gemstones and all the myriads of color one could possibly imagine, Charles described their origins, and I found myself wishing that he was describing them and placing them all over my naked body at that moment. What a beautiful picture that would create, don't you think?

In anticipation of his arrival, I had prepared some liqueur and hors d'ouevres. The more we drank, the closer we got, until Charles was putting the olives on the hors d'ouevres and feeding them to me, as I did to him reciprocally. He had a very sensual way of putting an hors d'ouevres in my mouth, and I in turn licked my upper lip in a very sensual way to turn him on. We both knew what we were doing right then and there.

At that moment, he told me, "I really like you. I like you a lot."

I said, "I really like you, too, Charles. I really do. We're gonna have some fun together, I know it."

Little did I know how involved he was going to get with me. He didn't give me a clue the rest of his visit. He was a complete gentleman as he explained that all of those gemstones, especially the aquamarines, came from a mine in Brazil that he owned. I'd never seen anything quite like them; they were rough cut gems, not polished. The aquamarines were very important to me because it is my birthstone, so I really wanted to have them with me in my bed when I went to sleep that night. They weren't very large, but they were large enough I knew that the energy that would be drawn to them would be absolutely amazing for me.

I then proceeded to ask him in a very thoughtful way if I could have them for the night. I told him I would like to keep them with me when I slept, that it would be very important for me.

"Of course," he said.

I was very surprised at his quick response, but then again I was learning more about him, and that was gorgeous.

On a warm summer night following our first meeting, Charles returned. We were outside in the garden, the air full of the smell of roses, very delicious and inviting to both of us. We were enjoying the lovely dinner that I had prepared, and as I had another glass of wine, I thought of how wonderful it would be to invite him to make love to me right there in the exquisite garden.

Before I could share those thoughts with him, he looked to me and said, "Susan, I want to make love to you now. Right now, here in the garden."

He took my hand and led me down to a beautiful area where flowers are abundant and the fragrance is delicious. He kissed me and slipped my panties down so that I could just step out of them.

Charles wasted no time; he just bent over me and we made love au naturel for hours. It was gorgeous, truly gorgeous, he had a beautiful brown body that he really took good care of, and oh my, did he use it to take good care of me! His wet kisses eventually led to his licking me all over, then sucking on my nipples and devouring me with his tongue in every way. His delicious cock was so comfortable in my mouth, and I sucked on him until he couldn't stand not being inside of me.

He said, "Please Susan, I need to go there right now. I need to feel your warm pussy wrapped around my 'so good for you hard cock'."

He quickly put a pillow from the garden chair down among the flowers, so that I could be on my knees, and he slowly and gently entered my wet pussy from behind. I couldn't wait to feel him inside of me. He cupped my voluptuous breasts, reaching them from behind as he pressed his wonderful body against me, with his gorgeous cock deep inside me. We experienced heaven on earth, among the flowers, and we both reached the place that we needed to get to so easily. Our juices flowed out of us in an uninhibited moment, in the garden of sexual delights.

Every time after that when he would come over, we would have a little coffee, a little whatever, as if we cared what we were drinking, and we would go up to my bedroom and he would make a thorough exhibition of loving me up and I of him. He loved to watch me pleasure myself with a toy, or my fingers, and then join me himself in that moment of sexual heights. He's such a visual lover with me. What a turn on and what a good time we always had.

The funny thing is, as long as Charles and I got together, he would always ask the same question. "I did a good job, didn't I? Tell me, Susan. I did a good job, I took good care of you, yes?"

And I always said, "Oh yes, Charles, oh yes, you always do. You're a beautiful gem yourself!"

What a guy, what a wonderful guy.

Arthur Johnson II

Is there a Mr. Arthur Johnson II in the house? Oh yes, there is, and when there first was, it took my breath away.

One day I was in a lower part of the city with my girlfriend having dinner when I noticed, standing at the bar, an amazing looking specimen of a man. He was tall, well built, and (ladies do notice such things) impeccably dressed and wearing a beautiful tie. The tie alone had such drama going on I couldn't resist going over and complimenting him on its exquisite pattern. All those moments about his look, his tie, and our meeting paved the way for us to get together at some point soon.

Arthur was very pleased with our conversation and, little by little, we got to know each other. From that first moment in the bar, it was obvious we would get together at some point. The conversation about the tie led to a discussion of his home with a lot of Liberty of London fabric. Learning I was a designer, he tried to impress me with his expertise in decorating. I must admit, he did know what he was talking about.

In addition to that, he was also the head of finance for a very prestigious university. Suitably impressed, I suggested we have a deeper discussion some time, and then I went back to finish the evening with my friend.

It wasn't long before Arthur and I went out. We had dinner several times in the city, and he began revealing to me that there were some very high-class women that he associated with that were into a wilder sexual side of life, and that if I ever wanted to watch or participate, that would be okay with him. What a thoughtful and kinky guy.

Though I was titillated, I declined, but eventually Arthur came to my home and we began to explore each other with sexual intentions. As things got heated, he reminded me what he'd told me about his cock, that it was so large most women wouldn't even be able to wrap their mouths around the head of it.

I'd laughed that off the first time I heard it, but when I first saw Arthur standing naked before me, I was glued to the spot, staring with amazement. I had to step back to take in the full view of him, because he had the biggest cock I had ever seen!

Not only was it thick and long, it was oh so velvety to the touch. The head of it was like a huge Portobello mushroom. It was so interesting to look at, the way that he encouraged the head to expand and contract like a camera lens. It was very velvety and malleable to the touch. It was quite the visual exhibition and exception to the rule. Damn! He'd warned me that a lot of women couldn't handle it; I'd thought he was exaggerating, but oh no, no, no.

I started slowly, very slowly, caressing him and taking my time, which got my own juices flowing very nicely.

With each stroke of Arthur's masterful cock, I felt more comfortable. Then he began returning the favor, searching me out with his fingers, coaxing my juices to begin to pour out of me. When he gently placed me onto my bed, he brushed his manly magnificence against my erect nipples while licking my ears and kissing my mouth. I was getting comfortable with the thought of our bodies merging. Finally, I felt that he could gently, ever so gently, begin to enter me.

Little by little, I was able to accommodate him. He filled me up as completely as possible. We'd taken our sweet delicious time, and his massive size wasn't a problem any longer. Arthur was thoughtful and gentle in making love to me, and when he brought me to climax, it was powerful, secretions pouring out of me like a river running to the sea.

Arthur Johnson II had the biggest cock that I ever did see. This man was packing, if you know what I mean. Damn! He had great taste, he tasted great, and guess what? He never envisioned the paradise that awaited him; quite the moment in my bed.

Christopher LaRoux

One summer's day, I decided to go to a clothing optional beach that I had visited before. I had a new foldout aluminum lounge designed to lay flat on. It was brand new, and I'm not terribly mechanical, so I thought I did a great job just opening it up and getting it assembled. As I put lotion on my body I was naked, as was everyone around me. Like I said, the beach was clothing optional, and I did the optional thing.

I laid down on my new lounge, flat on my belly so I could get a little color on my back, and the whole thing suddenly folded in half! I landed on the beach got sand all over me; it stuck to my body because I had lotioned up. It was the most awkward moment I'd felt in a very long time.

"That was quite something else what you just did," came a resonant male voice.

I looked up and saw a very attractive gentleman—not my type at the time, but soon to become my type—looking down at me and smiling.

"It was ridiculous," I said.

"Well, it looked good from here."

The conversation continued. I left the folded aluminum behind and we took a stroll on the beach. I quickly discovered he was quite thoughtful about everything. To my surprise, he didn't come on to me in a way that was obnoxious in any way. We walked and walked, talking non-stop. What was amazing was that he was a George Clooney look-alike, only much younger, but with the salt-and-pepper hair nonetheless.

His name was Christopher LaRoux. He lived in another state, and was originally from Paris. At the time, he was residing in an area several hours from my home.

By that night, he knew a few things about me, and I guess he liked what he'd learned because he called me.

Only I hadn't given him my number!

"How did you do this?" I asked when I heard his voice. "I'm not listed and you didn't even know what state I was living in!"

"Don't worry, I know my things," he replied, chuckling. He told me he worked with computers a lot, and was very resourceful. I would find out just how amazingly resourceful later.

So we made arrangements and he wanted to come visit me. I said that would be great, but not that night. I was looking forward to it, but things kept coming up. In the interim, we spent a lot of time communicating via the computer. We emailed each other constantly when he had time, and when I could I responded. We were both very busy—it was frustrating to both of us.

One day during the back and forth emails he suggested something I'd never thought of—using web cams.

I already had one, because of a friend in another country. She and I, someone I knew from high school, communicated that way.

Christopher's email gave me a thrill when I read it:

Did you ever experience cybersex?

I responded honestly:

No, I haven't.

He called me and said, "Well, guess what? We're going to try that."

Damn! It was amazing! It was so sensual, watching him masturbate. He watched me. He kept his audio off because he was married (not happily, obviously). As I watched him cum, throwing his head back with his mouth open, I typed a message:

Was that a silent scream that you had when you reached a climax?

He looked at the camera and grinned. He didn't have to say, "Yes, it was."

That was the first time I'd ever participated in anything like that, and it was fun. Earlier in my life, I would have been a little hesitant about men. I would have worried over whether I was going to miss a phone call. I might have felt I had to stay home for two nights in a row so as to not miss a phone call. I'd had so many times of, maybe it'll happen, and maybe it wouldn't.

Now, everything was *instant*! I remember watching him masturbating and I heard a noise from the other room—my dryer hand finished its cycle and my clothes were dry. I typed out that I would be back. I left the area for a minute and went and folded the clothes. When the laundry was completely put away, I came back, and he was still masturbating!

Boy, how I have changed, I thought. *I have changed my ways, baby!*

As Christopher reached climax for himself he came right on the floor in his studio room office space, and I remembered he had mentioned telling his wife he was watching a baseball game there. What would happen, I wondered, if his wife came in and saw him masturbating to a baseball game, how weird would that be?!

When I mentioned that thought to him later on the phone, the whole sexy thing suddenly became very funny. It was just one example of many of how we were having such a good time.

Another night we did the same thing but I'd learned it was very odd for me to be in front of a camera like that and not have any audio. So I asked him to go outside when he was done climaxing. Say he was walking the dog, walking a bird, anything, and when he was there, talk to me from outside the house and bring me to climax. And he certainly did! I would touch myself, excited by his voice and the things he would tell me about what he would like to do to me, and I would reach a fabulous climax. He was quite the guy.

The other thing about Christopher was that before the next time he came to my house, I did a painting on black paper, with beautiful brushstrokes of color and using gold leaf foil. I wrote on it, Cum As You Are. "How about we do a little special tribute," I said when I showed it to him. "It's like this, I love that you love me to watch you get off, so why don't we memorialize that? You can masturbate and cum on this painting that I've prepared for you."

He grinned and began taking off his pants. I put the painting on the floor and he took care of that for me, with a little encouragement from me. It was so giving and wonderful of him, and I thanked him for the effort. Now I had my very own personal art apprentice.

"Now you have my DNA," he said.

"Please," I said. "It's nothing, it's little. It's so beautiful and liquidy, it belongs and enhances the painting!"

Some time later, I asked for him to do it again, for my birthday. I handed him a new painting that I already prepared for this occasion. "This is my birthday card," I said. "Would you do that for me again?"

And he did, even better than the last time. The man has talent!

We've taken showers together and he does whatever I ask him because I don't ask him for anything too outrageous. We have a lot of fun and he's going to be in my life for a long long time. Yes, Christopher LaRoux loves to amaze me.

One of Christopher's other major gifts to me is that he adores my body. He tells me it's so exquisite. He adores my derriere, my breasts, and he honors me with continuous compliments that I love very much because they make me feel totally free. I can just be myself with him. I don't have to hide anything or feel shy about anything. He's made me the most uninhibited woman and I love him for that.

So here's to you, Christopher! You have a body that is exquisite as well. You keep saying you have to lose 20 pounds, and I keep telling you, you do that and we're done.

Just kidding, of course.

I've happily cooked many meals for him. He's a very simple eater, very simple tastes, meat and potatoes. But I keep trying to do better for him, making a nice salad once, some lamb chops, and he told me he adored my expanding his culinary horizons. Another time we had chicken with vegetables and he loved that, too.

Christopher is comfortable with me in every way as I am with him. I see him about once every month, sufficient for both of us for now, because when it is that time, the experience is so filled with beauty and sex and gorgeousness that all the other three weeks that remain hold lingering memories, good times reflecting on all the delicious moments we've spent together.

From being with him, I'm not a needy woman any more. Thank God!

The most important element of Christopher is that he brings me to climax by touching me in a way that no one else has ever done. With his fingers inside of me, his fingers on my clitoris, he can do the ultimate every time for me, giving me tremendous joy and pleasure and release of emotions.

Not only that, he's a master at massage. He gives me a two-hour deeply caressing sensual massage, prior to even getting involved in a sexual nature. It's just beautiful. We're both naked on a beautiful flannel duvet cover I spread on the soft carpeted floor. Somehow, he knows how to masterfully touch and massage me to send me into throes of ecstasy. He's a master sensualist, not a massage therapist, but he might as well be as far as I'm concerned. He's wonderful, wonderful.

Most importantly, we're so honest with each other it maintains an open, free relationship, easy come, easy go. Or should I say, easy cum, easy as it goes? Yeah, baby, either way, it's the best.

Delicious David

My All-Time Favorite Lover, All-Time Favorite Soulmate for Life, is Mr. David O'Neal. Finally, I met a man with a sense of sexual adventure equal to my own!

I met him when I was working with a female jazz great. His aunt was the stylist for her. He was coming into the city where my client was performing, and as she told me about him, a warm smile began to light up her face. I say began, since she caught herself quickly saying, "If only you were younger you would be perfect for my nephew."

What she didn't know was how right she was and how, despite our ages, how perfect he and I were going to be.

Oh my. The first night we met, David, his aunt, and I went to a lovely French restaurant for some dinner. It was simply delicious. She suggested that we continue enjoying the night, taking in some jazz, exploring the clubs and hot spots in the city. She said that she was tired and would be going back to the hotel, and retiring to bed for the night.

We both decided to take her up on her suggestions, wishing her a good night. We enthusiastically encouraged her since we already knew that this night was going to be the beginning of something amazing.

The feeling of comfort and curiosity began as we shared stories in a taxi, on the way to an intimate jazz club downtown in the heart of the city. Somehow, we felt as though we'd known each other for years, and magically the unbridled sexual energy started flying. We wound up at an intimate jazz club in a remote area of the city. After we were seated, we found our fingers intertwined then gently separating for just a moment, in order to caress each other's legs under the table. Oh how good that felt, the prelude to what awaited us. He was staying at the hotel where his aunt was, and I was going to return to my own home that night. I returned with him to his hotel to wish him a good night, and to pick up my design portfolio that I had left in his aunt's room. He told me that he wanted to make love to me right at that moment, on the steps leading out from the corridor on each floor. I told him that I wasn't interested in participating in something that was quite that spontaneous, but as time does tell, hotter and more "in the moment" times soon developed.

David and I were inevitable. The moments that followed our first meeting were simply amazing because he is a very sexual, very frisky, and very wild and crazy man! And at the same time, he's a whole lot of fun. We literally turn each other on like fountains of water, sensation flowing between us like nothing else I have ever experienced. He achieves sexual arousal so easily for me because of his amazing sense of touch. This man knows my body in ways that go beyond familiar. His professional career is as a very big deal in the world of very expensive gemstones and as a result, his schedule is very demanding, but he has repeatedly taken time out to be with me, whenever we can match our schedules. Having him is like savoring a rare wine that makes me feel warm and uninhibited with imaginative thoughts of savoring past moments with him, and creating new scenarios of plans to come.

One evening, I did something very creative, something he told me he would never forget. I took some black gauze fabric and placed Velcro on the frame of each car window, in order to create our own magical paradise on the inside of my car. When I met David in the city, he had no idea what I had in mind for us, and I didn't let on as we drove to an isolated location. We parked in an area that you might call desolate, near the docks of the city.

As I gracefully put together the tent of sheer dark fabric and then began removing my silk blouse, David couldn't hold back and began caressing my full breasts. My nipples were becoming erect, waiting for his wonderful warm mouth to suck on them. We made love in the car, steaming the windows, ruffling the fabric like billowing sails of passion with sighs and exhalations in our deeply passionate sex. Oh my god, we were laughing and playing and kissing and loving and having such a good time.

The way I'd constructed the curtains, no one could see in, but we could see out. It was very creative of me, if I must say, and he loved it. We made up our minds this was something to do again, and again!

David had his own creativity, which I found even more exciting. Once, he took me to a prestigious restaurant in the city, that naturally, I can't name (in case we ever want to go back), and for most of the meal I thought it was just a pleasant dinner, but David had something special in mind for dessert. In a secluded hallway, you see, there was a phone booth with mahogany paneling on the door that was waist high, with two tall panes of glass on top. Standing outside the phone booth, you couldn't really see what was going on—at least, in the bottom half of the booth.

I couldn't understand why he wanted me with him to make a phone call, and he didn't explain until we were standing outside the booth.

"Let's go in there," he said. "I need to make a call."

"You are a really wild and crazy guy," I said, smiling. "What kind of call?"

"You'll just have to see, won't you? Trust me."

Before I knew what was happening, he had me inside the booth, standing between him and the phone as he gently slipped my panties down. His pants were open, his cock was hard, and he asked me to reach behind and feel it. It was rock hard, and before I knew it he was sliding deep inside of me. I felt his hard, erect, thick member enter my wet pussy as he stood behind me, thrusting slowly, rhythmically in and out. He moved even more closely against me, subtly as he could, taking care to not alert anyone who might be walking by. Then, to my surprise, he reached over my shoulder to the front of the phone, picked up the receiver, deposited some coins, and dialed a number.

By now, he was breathing so heavily. He had me hold the receiver to my ear, and an answering machine came on. It was his personal answering machine at his office. As I clutched the phone to my ear, we continued our wild embraces. We left the phone off the hook and continued our lovemaking, every moan, every word, every joyful moment, sexual expletives, cries of passion, everything recorded remotely, the entire time that he was having sex with me in the booth.

It was *amazing*. I don't know how we got so lucky, but no one walked by, no one knew what we'd done, and we walked out into the hallway like nothing more had happened than our just being on the phone. It was very exciting to have surreptitious sex in a place known for its elegance, high-end clientele, and rather well appointed surroundings. It was a caper that only the daring could pull off, and absolutely amazing that no one had a clue. A high five on that one, baby. We went back to our table and casually ordered dessert.

If I thought that little caper was astonishing, David had something even better in mind. He came over to my place a few weeks later and just as we were deep in the throes of a very heated moment, he took the receiver off the cradle of my bedroom phone, and said, "Let me dial my office."

Without interrupting our passionate moment, he reached his answering machine, hit a couple of numbers on my phone, and I was amazed at what I heard over the speaker. There we were, having wild and crazy sex again, this time in my bedroom, in my bed, and what did I hear over the phone? It was the whole continued conversation from the restaurant phone booth, and as though we were right there again, taking all sorts of chances in our crazily daring sensual adventure!

It was like making love in stereo! Oh, did we have a good, good time with that one.

I never knew what would be in store with Mr. O'Neal. Once, I picked him up from his residence on a very cold snowy morning. It was 5:00 a.m. and he was going to work, and I'd brought along an amazing breakfast for him that I prepared myself. He insisted that we were running well ahead of schedule, and he wanted to stop and have a nice breakfast with me, alone. So wouldn't you know it, we found a nicely secluded spot, a dead-end off a dirt road, and we sat there having hot buttered corn muffins dripping with jelly, drinking coffee and getting hotter for each other with each passing moment. We worked each other up into a sexual frenzy, touching each other all over, in every possible spot on our bodies until we couldn't take it any more.

We got out of the car and I leaned against the side of the car with David positioned behind me. We kept our winter clothing on but for some reason I intentionally forgot to wear any panties. It was very fortunate I was thoughtful enough to be absent-minded, because David unzipped his pants and took out his beautiful hot black cock and slid it inside of my warm wet pussy, in a way that made me quiver with delight as the snowflakes were falling down around us. The contrast of the cold outside and the warmth of our bodies against and inside each other as we loved each other up in the snow, was beyond amazing. In a flash of moments, we went from having hot corn muffins with butter and jelly to having the craziest early morning wake-up sex ever, outside leaning on my car. What a feast, what a ride that was, without moving a mile.

Yes, Mr. O'Neal had a thing about abandoned dirt roads. By most people's estimate, it was difficult to have sex in the car in the city without getting interrupted, but we'd had such wonderful experiences, we thought it would always be quite safe. Since we both lived a little further away from each other than was comfortable for easy visits, one night we sort of met in the middle, geographically. And very shortly thereafter, we met in the middle intimately. There we were in the car, David's pants down around his knees. Once again, I had come to him wearing nothing under my skirt, my panties left at home. We were touching each other all over. He was massaging my nipples, sucking on my voluptuous breasts. It was ecstasy, when all of a sudden a bright light came shining through the window. Oh yes it did!

David and I were both pretty well known in our communities, which made our situation *very* precarious. That wasn't just any bright light; it was a police flashlight! We began whispering frantically about what might happen, oh my, oh my.

Except the policeman didn't seem particularly perplexed. "Excuse moi," he said casually as David rolled down his window slightly. Was that a hint of amusement I heard in the officer's voice? "Excuse me," the policeman continued. "What are you folks doing here like this?"

"We started out watching stars and talking, officer," I explained. "I guess we just got a little carried away!"

"A little?" replied the officer. Outside, the officer was simply nodding. His flashlight mainly focused on our faces and, giving us a moment to get ourselves together, he said, "I would take that elsewhere if I were you. I would be on your way, right now. Okay?"

I started my car while David was trying to put his pants back on. David said. "We'll have to canvas other geographic options."

I felt myself start breathing again when I saw the officer walk back toward his car, and when he got in the driver's seat and shut the door, David and I both commented at the same time, "That was a close call!"

"We're not going to do this kind of stuff again," David said, watching me get dressed. He smiled. "Not that I didn't enjoy it!"

"Me, too," I replied, buttoning my blouse. "But we could have been splashed all over the newspapers for tomorrow morning's early reading. Wouldn't that have been one for the books?"

But it was great as always.

Mr. David O'Neal, such a wild and crazy guy, so endlessly sexual. The more we got to know each other, the more I learned about him, and some times his stories made my head swim. He'd had many experiences of multiple women partners with him at the same time. He'd call up a woman or two that he knew for a foursome, along with his cousin Norman, and other times perhaps another male friend with him and another woman, when he felt the need to feel erotically inspired. There were so many detailed escapades that I always felt privileged to hear, every last one of them, eagerly drinking in every last drop of every single detail.

There's no doubt that David is a sex addict and he loves being that. I love that about him because he's free enough to experience everything, along with being brilliant and inventively sexual and thoughtful and fun with me every time. We have our separate sexual experiences and I look forward to sharing my exploits with him when we get together, so that we're on the same page with each other's lives. I don't go in the same direction as he does with a lot of things, but he knows he can tell me about every last thing without my judging what he does.

Our trust is so deep he once permitted me to take photographs of him and his beautiful erect cock when he was at my home. I love thinking about it to this day, and I look at the pictures for inspiration whenever I find myself needing to relive some kind of moment, or if I'm just thinking of him. In one picture, David is beautiful with his gorgeous white teeth, his personality shining like the sun. In another, his tongue licks his upper lip in a sexually suggestive way, like he has done with me many times. In another he's holding his cock out with his hand, showing me how ready he is for me, always. I love what he has done for me, opening me up this way, such a sweetheart. I love him a lot.

When I took the pictures, I asked him if it would be okay to use the exquisite photographs to pleasure myself.

"Of course," he said. "You know I do, and I know you will!"

In order to accomplish the final step in this surreptitious feat of creativity I had to locate a place that would have the ability to transfer them from my high resolution digital camera to actual photographs. I arrived at the place where I could accomplish this labor of love mission. As I positioned myself in front of the machine, I began the process by following the instructions on the screen before me. First I had to insert my American Express credit card into the slot, then I proceeded to remove the digital chip from my camera which contained all of my photo images of the last six months, including the specific ones that I needed now. There were photos of my garden, my cats, and everything else. After being instructed to insert the chip into the correct slot, I had to scroll through all of the photos, until lo and behold, there before me were David's photos with his smile, his cock, his wonderful hand holding his cock for me, all clearly displayed on the screen. I immediately draped my entire body over the machine's viewer, in order to hide these very personal X-rated images from all of the regulars who were there to make copies of architectural plans, children's handprints for family calendars, poems for school projects, and whatever else the average person that comes through those doors uses those photocopying machines for.

Now that the choices were available to me, I had to select the size that I wanted them to be printed in. My mind was being very creative thinking, "Can you imagine blowing them up to poster size with some hot sexy captions underneath?" Just a crazy and wild thought, but wouldn't it be amazing! Back to reality, I chose the not so small size of 5x7, thinking that would be perfect for me to look at, to encourage myself with and hold in my hand whenever I needed to call upon them for those extra special moments, if you can get that. Once again, I had to act with split-second timing. In one fell swoop, I had to quickly extract the photos as they instantly dropped into another slot where they were delivered from the machine to me. Wow! I've now officially become the "Drape and Shield" expert for naughty triple X-rated photos.

And that's exactly what has happened. I love it, I love it, my own personal David O'Neal photo porn collection.

We have continued to experience wonderful things every time we come together. Not only do I have his pictures, his presence with me is so fully alive I can recall every pant, every moan, how he has felt inside of me at so many wild, hot moments when we both expressed every erotic sound with expletives that totally and specifically describe our volcanic lovemaking. And to top it off, I have this extra special moment with David when I decided to pleasure him like he's never been pleasured before. Once when he returned to my Palace of Paradise again, and we had begun to touch and explore each other with our usual sexual passion, I asked him to just stand before me and close his eyes. Of course he trusted me, and knew that this was going to be something amazing. I rubbed my hands together briskly so as to encourage heat, with a wonderful lubricating cream. I then gently applied the cream to his magnificent cock, rubbing it in slow circular motions, so that he'd be prepared for what was to be next. I had the most beautiful long strand of cultured pearls that I so gently wrapped around the shaft of his cock, leaving the head free to be soothed and stimulated by me as well. Holding his not yet fully erect cock in my warm hands, I gently rotated the pearls on the shaft as I rubbed the head with my free hand.

The erotic feeling that this gave to him made him cry out with sheer joy, and his breathing became faster and faster, until he said, "Please stop, please stop, I can't take another second of this feeling of compete ecstasy, it's going to be too much for me to handle!"

By that time, his 8-1/2 inch cock had reached its full potential, and we were ready to take care of business, as they say. Damn, do I have the power, or what?!

David O'Neal, you are a wild, creative, crazy, and fabulous guy. I love you for all that we have been through together, all those things we have done together, and everything that we will share together in the future. You are amazing!

In Closing

I've learned a lot from love, and one of the biggest things is that I will never grow out of being playful and fun loving. I will always be a sensual woman, always practicing safe sex, because my body is my temple. I'm just having a great time, just as I have for decades. I hope people have the freedom to explore life like I have. To touch on that freedom, I must add that the other day when I was driving in my car, I decided to listen to a track on my CD titled "The Last Time" sung by the great Cee Lo Green. Not giving it a second thought, I pulled over, flung open the car door, and started moving and grooving to the fabulous beat, as well as listening to his lyrics. I was dancing up a storm right outside of my car. I didn't care who was passing by, or if they noticed. The percussive sounds while he sang were amazingly persuasive, and I was so inspired by that moment that I got back in my car, and immediately drove to a music store and picked up a tambourine and some ankle bells, so that I could continue to move with bells around my bare feet, creating rhythmical sounds that were beyond belief.

That night, I placed votive candles everywhere, illuminating my home for an exquisite and dramatic ambiance, as I danced for my lover. Thank you, Cee Lo, you are an amazing inspiration to me. I would love to meet and design for you, since you've touched my creative soul. I understand your passion, I feel it, and I love it. To be in touch with you would be like the lavender icing on my red velvet cake. You are truly Red Velvet.

Now that I've reached the age of 70, I can say that I've indulged in a great many experiences in life that have given me wonderful pleasure, whether it's sexual or otherwise, and I will continue to take that path because it keeps me very young and feeling vibrant and allows me to continue on the path of rejuvenation.

I'm constantly reflecting on my past experiences and looking forward to new ones. I remain thoughtful, caring, safe, and sizzlingly sexy and hot. I wish my kind of enthusiasm for anyone who chooses to go in that direction and enjoy life the way I have.

I want to add that I've been fortunate that the men in my life have always adored my body. I am voluptuous. I am sensual. I am Rubenesque, and soft to the touch. My lips are full and soft and, I've been told, "good for kissing." On a scale of one to ten, I'd say that I'm an eleven. I accept myself totally. Everything about me is very feminine, and the wonderful men I have known have encouraged me to feel that way about myself, much more so than I would have done on my own. I love that about these men. They've cherished me, and I in return cherish myself even more.

So thank you, men, you've really done me justice, and here are some lines that I wrote, especially for you. *All of you!*

Your smile that illuminates the exterior of your soul touches me, like droplets of moonbeams on a clear summer night.

How the caress of your skin inspires warmth and wetness deep within the crevices of my passion.

Oh yes, I could reach out before me and touch the quiet of the moment, and at the same time feel the warmth and caress of you beside me.

Pressing, rubbing, moving ever so rhythmically against the contours of my body, your hands caressingly discovering my breasts, my nipples anxious to feel the warmth of your mouth upon them.

Oh, how I love how you do that. Your skin so moist to my touch, your body so smooth and delicious. How I love all that.

Your body so aroused with strength and passion and wetness. How wonderful it is for me to run my hands along the contours of your delicious body, seeking out special places where my hands and mouth find sweet pleasures. And you, in all of your manly sensual magnificence, explore the feminine wilds of me, the wetness, the fragrance of my skin, the rhythm of my body as you search out the deepest,

97

warmest crevices of wetness with your fingers.

How good that feels, oh yes, don't stop. To feel you deep inside my soul, to share that moment, is the ultimate specialness between us. Oh yes, it's all true. That moment has just touched on beautiful. I feel you in my heart. I feel you in my soul.

I love you.